# THIS BOOK BELONG TO:

..............................................................

..............................................................

www.ingramcontent.com/pod-product-compliance
Lightning Source LLC
Chambersburg PA
CBHW081600270726
48657CB00029B/3441